ISBN: 978-0-578-77628-6
LCCN: 2020919133

This book belongs to
_____ a fashionista.

Aa

Fashionista's
wear aprons

A is for Apron

B is for Bow

C c C c C c C c

c   c

c   c

c      c

c   c

c   c

c   c

C c C c C c C c

Fashionista

26 New
Fashion Trends

Fashion Week
Top Runway Looks

Beautiful, Confident, & Smart

C is for Cover Girl

D is for Dress

Ee

E is for Earrings

F is for Fashion Show

Gg

G is for Glass Slipper

H is for Hat

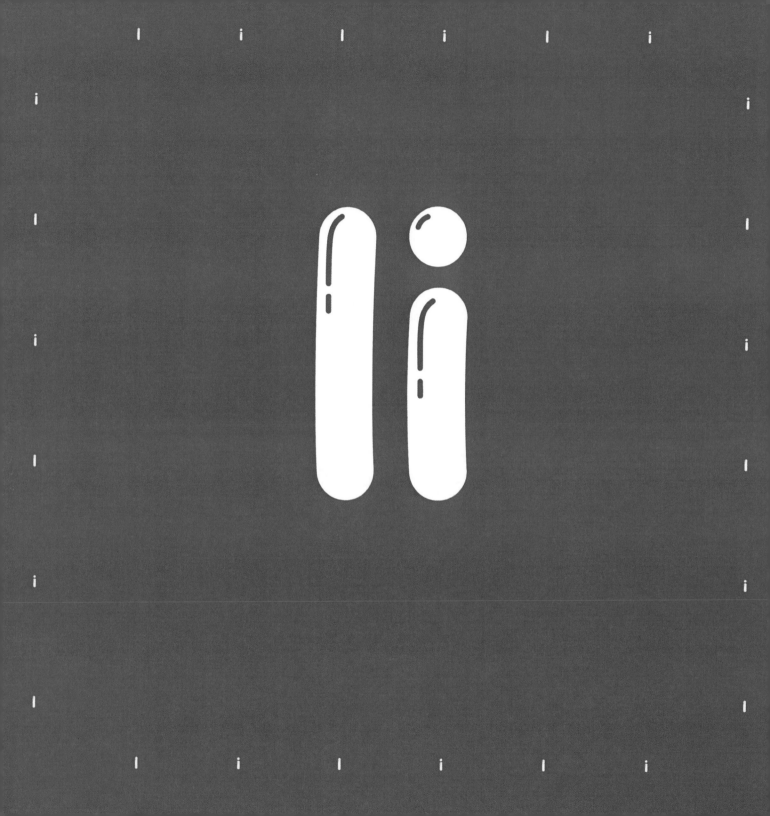

I is for Ice Skates

J is for Jumpsuit

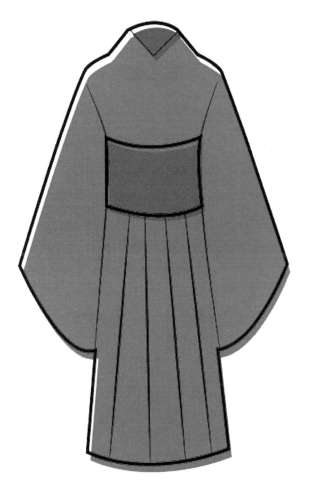

K is for Kimono

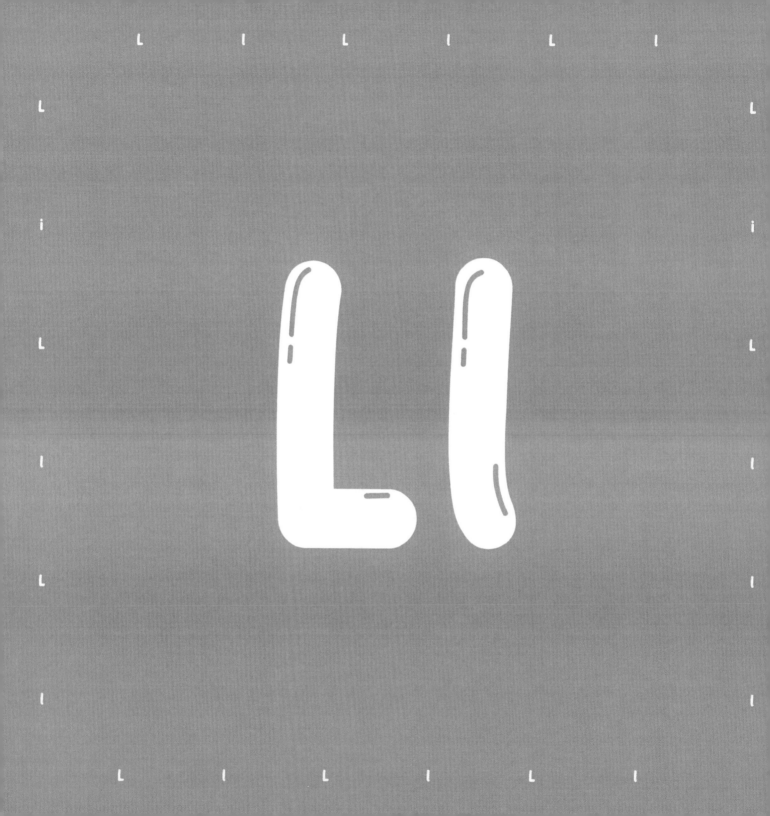

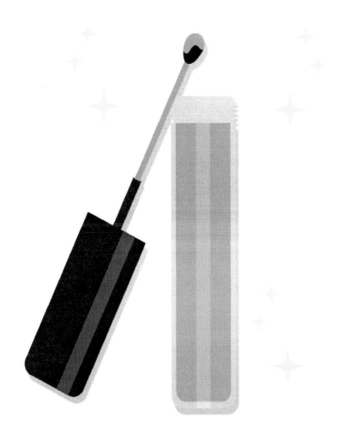

L is for Lipgloss

Mm

M is for Model

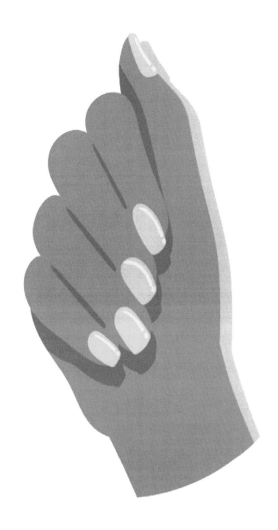

N is for Nail

O is for Overcoat

P is for Purse

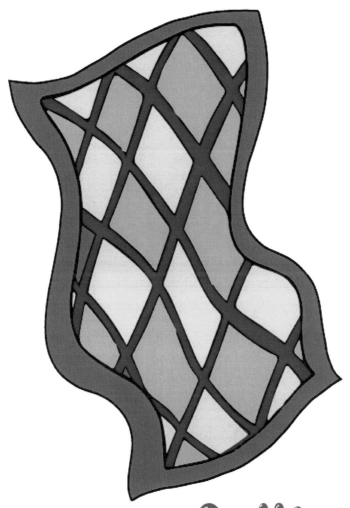

Q is for Quilt

R is for Rainboots

S is for Swimsuit

Tt

T is for Tiara

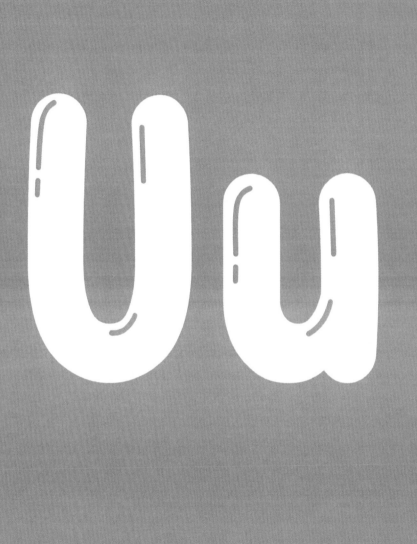

U is for Umbrella

V is for Vest

Ww

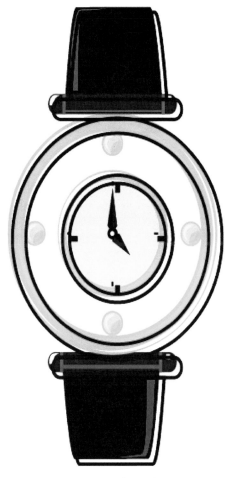

W is for Watch

X is for Xray Glasses

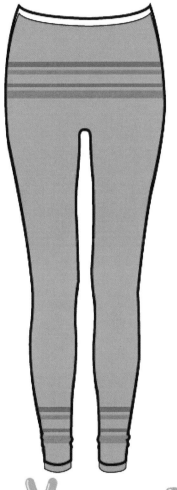

Y is for Yoga Pants

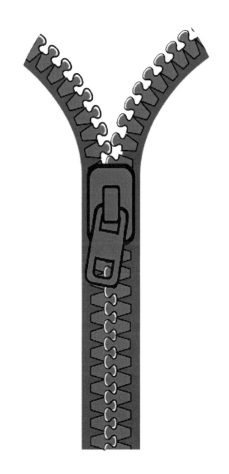

Z is for Zipper

Made in United States
North Haven, CT
28 September 2023